Written by Omeaka Jackson

# ANN MEETS M.RS. JONES

*A foster Care book for children*

Illustrated by Deg Philip & Devonna Arrington

Written by Omeaka Jackson

Illustrated by Deg Philip
& Devonna Arrington

# ANN MEETS MRS. JONES

*A foster Care book for children*

# Dedication

This book is dedicated to my children, bonus daughter, Sweet Jayla, all the children who have been and are in foster care. A special thank you to foster parents who open up their hearts, homes, and families to children who are in need and fostering care.

I gift this book to

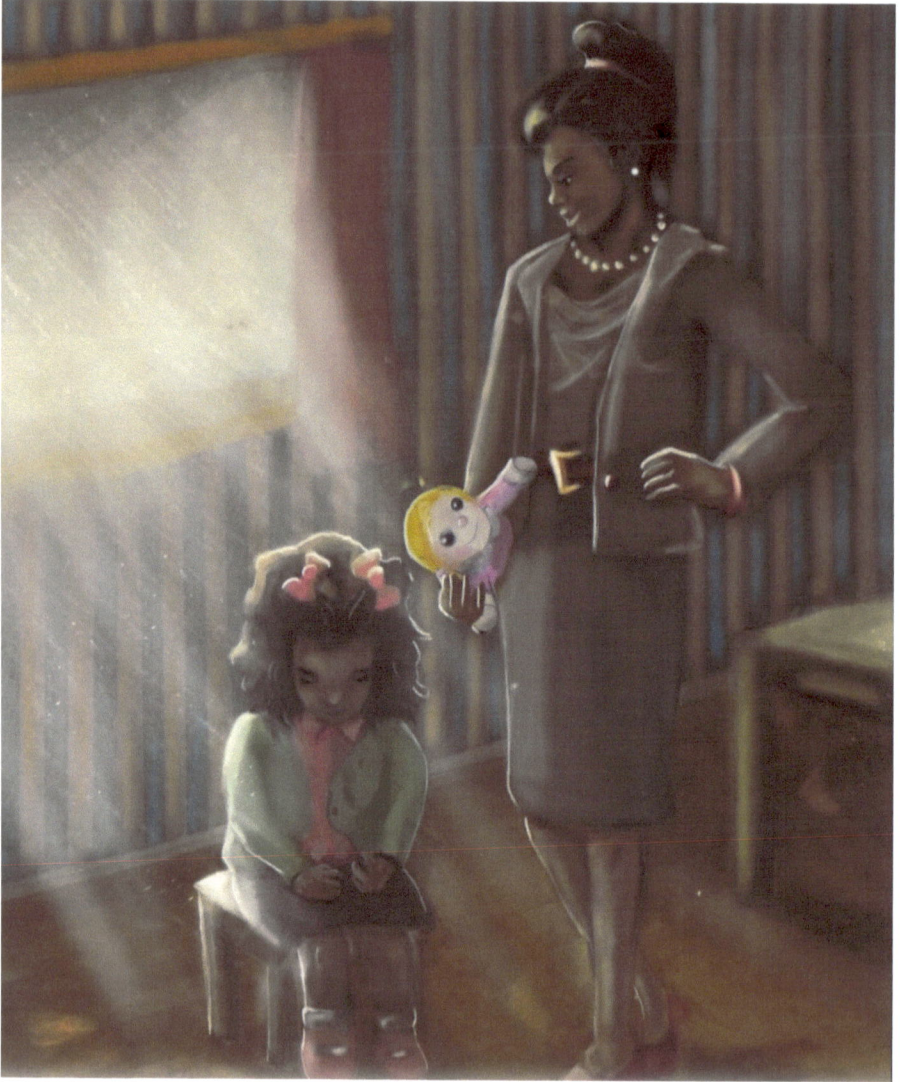

"How are you doing Ann? I know your social worker just left but I want to make sure you are ok. " Mrs. Jones says.

"I'm ok I guess. What is a foster mother, "Ann replies?

"A foster parent is someone who takes care of children who are removed from their parent's or guardian's care, or does not have an adult who can care for them," Mrs. Jones, explains.

"I don't want a new parent. I want my mommy and daddy," Ann says looking down with her face in her hands.

"I'm not here to replace your parents. I am a foster parent to you. That means I'm here to provide support, love, and guidance. I provide temporary care to children who are in foster care," Mrs. Jones replies.

"How long will I have to stay here? I really miss my family and my toys," Ann says.

"I'm not sure it depends on your parents, your social worker and the judge," Mrs. Jones replies.

"Oh!," Ann says, "Will I get to see my parents and my friends?"

"I'm not sure, but we can ask your social worker. Some children get weekly supervised visits, others get to visit on the weekend, and other have to wait. It depends on why children are in foster care and if their parents are working on the improvements that the judge told them to do," Mrs. Jones says.

"I don't know why I'm with you and not at home," Ann says.

"Ann I don't have all the information on why you were removed from your parents but when your social worker Ms. Johnson comes back today she may be able to tell us," Mrs. Jones responds.

"Do you have toys, will I have my own bed," asks Ann?

"Yes I have toys that you can play with and yes you will have your own bed in your own bedroom. Would you like to go see it now," Mrs. Jones responds with a smile?

Ann looks around the room, she sees all the toys and she smiles. She gets up on the bed with the doll. She is sad and starts to cry.

"Do want to tell me why you are crying Ann," Mrs. Jones asks?

Ann did not respond.

"I know it's scary to be with a stranger in a new house. I want you to know that Mr. Jones and I can help you. We can talk to you about your parents and your feelings. We know it's going to be hard but we are here to help you. Would you like that? "Yes sometimes," Ann said softly.

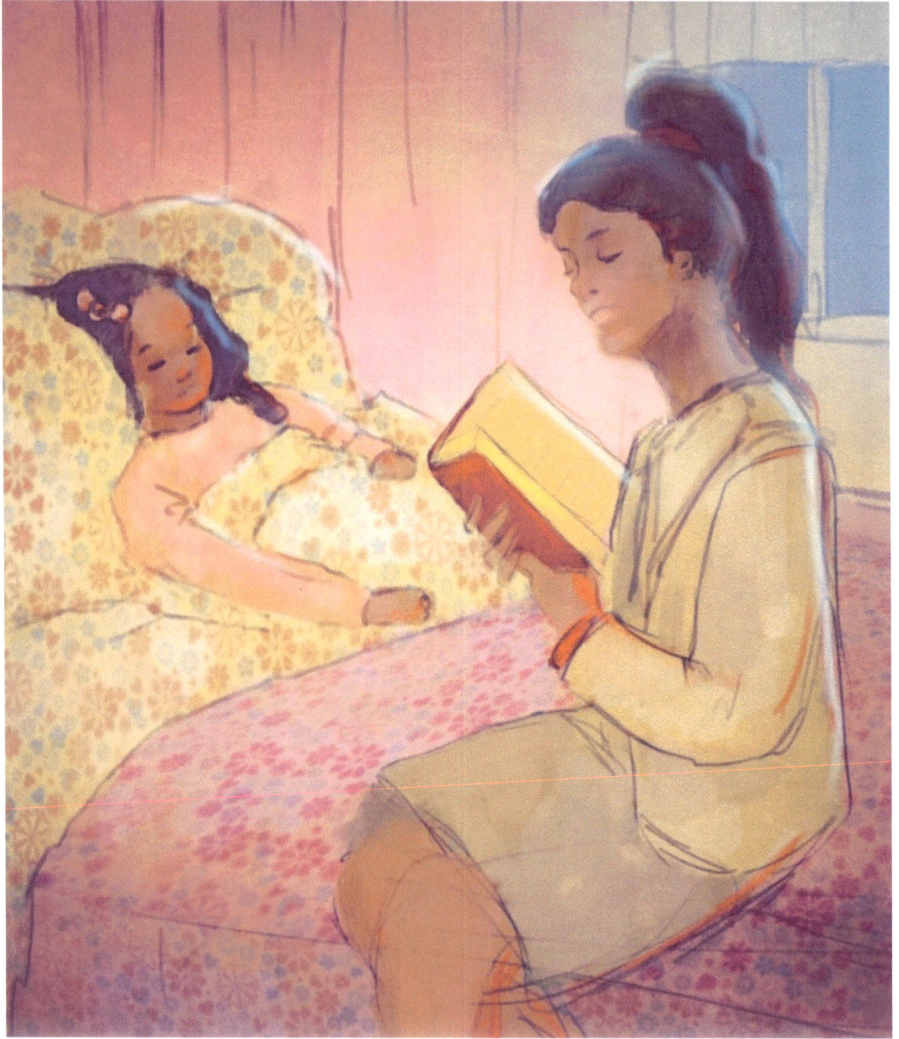

"I know it's going to be difficult at times, but I also know if we work together we can make it easier," Mrs. Jones said. "Is it ok if I give you a hug?" she asks. Ann shakes her head yes. Mrs. Jones asks if she's hungry and Ann says no. When asked if she would like her to read her a book she said yes. Ann fell asleep before Mrs. Jones finished the book.

# For Foster Parents

Remember children are taught to stay away from strangers, however being placed in foster care is the opposite of what we teach them. Remember you are a stranger to that child coming into your care.

It's very traumatic for children to be removed from their homes without notice and taken to a strange place with people they don't know.

It's natural for them to miss their biological families even other foster families.

Abuse and or neglect is why they are typically removed from their biological families care.

The children can display different types of emotions from anger, grief, loss, anxiety, or depression to name just a few. It all depends on the child and their life experiences.

Some of the children will have behavioral health issues due to abuse and neglect. It's important for them to be in treatment with a licensed clinical professional who can help them process what they have experienced and understand their emotions. This would include adjusting to a new home, new people, new school, new rules, etc.

Some behavioral health diagnosis they may have diagnosed or undiagnosed include but not limited to Posttraumatic Stress Disorder (PTSD), Reactive Attachment Disorder (RAD), Adjustment Disorder, Oppositional Defiance Disorder, Attachment Disorder, Depression, Anxiety. Again a licensed clinical professional can help with behavioral concerns.

Remember empathy and compassion is important and self-care.

If you notice the faces looking a bit different it's on purpose due to some children having the experience of being placed in multiple foster homes.

**Thank you for opening your hearts and homes to children who are in need of loving and caring homes!!**

## Resource Page

www.attachment.org/

www.attach.org/

www.instituteforattachment.ong/

www.futureofchildren.princeton.edu/

www.childmind.org

www.childwelfare.gov/

www.nfpaonline.org/

www.nctsn.org

## About the Author

Omeaka Jackson is a licensed clinical professional counselor. She is the founder and CEO of Harvesting Hope Youth and Family Wellness, Inc. A non-profit program for youth and families that provides behavior health counseling and youth and family development. She is the mother of 2 children and has one grandchild. She has a bonus daughter and 3 bonus grandchildren. She lives in Maryland.

Written by Omeaka Jackson

Illustrated by Deg Philip
& Deyanna Arrington

# ANN MEETS MRS. JONES

*A foster Care book for children*